W9-BHN-472

Have You Met My Divine Uncle George?

Patricia Wilson

The Upper Room
Nashville, Tennessee

Scripture quotations unless otherwise identified are from the *Good News Bible, The Bible in Today's English Version*, copyright by American Bible Society, 1966, 1971, © 1976, and are used by permission.

Scripture quotations designated RSV are from the Revised Standard Version of the Bible, copyrighted 1946, 1952, and © 1971 by the Division of Christian Education, National Council of the Churches of Christ in the United States of America, and are used by permission.

Scripture quotations designated KJV are from the King James Version of the Bible.

Book and Cover Design: Thelma Whitworth
First Printing: February, 1986 (5)
Library of Congress Catalog Card Number: 85-52016
ISBN: 0-8358-0529-8

Printed in the United States of America

For Gerald,
a gift from the heart

Contents

Introduction

The Giver of Gifts

---

*The Father will give you whatever
you ask of him in my name.*
—John 15:16

I used to have a little box sitting on my kitchen table. Inside the box, there was a card for every day of the year, and on each card was a "precious promise" from the Bible. Some days that promise was just what I needed to hear. On days when I knew there were trials ahead (an interview with Nathan's teacher), I would read that I could "do all things in him who strengthens me" (Phil. 4:13, RSV). On other days, when I was feeling exhausted and tired out, I would read, "Come unto me, all ye that labor and are heavy laden, and I will give you rest" (Matt. 11:28, KJV).

Over the year, I became aware of how many of these promises were actually gifts from God. The idea of God as a gift-giver is an intriguing one. Kierkegaard once suggested that Christians often picture God as a kind of divine "Uncle George," who dispenses gifts to his less fortunate relatives.

"Uncle George! How wonderful to see you. I'm so glad you could come."

"And I'm so pleased that you invited me."

"Where have you been visiting this time?"

"Oh, various places . . . the usual. You know how it is. Busy here, busy there."

"Your room is all ready for you. I put some fresh flowers in just this morning."

"That was very thoughtful of you. I've been thinking of you, too, and I've brought you a few small gifts."

"Oh, Uncle George. You shouldn't have!"

"Now, now. Giving gifts is a great pleasure for me. You must let me indulge myself. Here's a little something I know you'll like, and I remembered how much you enjoy these, and I'm sure that you must need some of this, especially right now. I didn't forget this little item, either, and I brought you another of these."

"Oh, Uncle George, I can't possibly take all this. How can I ever repay you?"

"Repay me? Nonsense. Just enjoy my gifts. That's repayment enough for me."

"Uncle George" is that larger than life character who bursts into our small, humdrum worlds, bringing gifts and benevolence, and leaving behind a fond memory which soon fades like a pleasant dream.

In whatever guise Uncle George may come to us, he is always characterized by his unbounding generosity. During his brief visits, he lavishes us with wonderful gifts. His generosity is all the more obvious because he doesn't expect anything in return.

For many Christians, God is little more than a divine Uncle George. This divine Uncle George isn't a permanent member of the family, but he is invited to visit briefly in times of need or stress, when he can be counted on to dispense heavenly benevolence. More importantly, his gifts are expected to be generous, with no expectation of anything more than a thank-you in return. Divine Uncle George is certainly not expected to outstay his welcome. When the gifts have been given out, when the crisis is over or the disaster has been averted, it is time for him to leave.

This perception of God as Divine Uncle George is not surprising. In many ways, Christians have been encouraged to think of God as some kind of super Santa Claus. In the beginning of a new relationship with Jesus, the zealous "converter" joyfully informs the "convertee" of the great benefits of the Christian life: "The Father will give you whatever you ask of him in my name" (John 15:16). No wonder the new Christian immediately starts making out a shopping list!

For some of us, Divine Uncle George is our only view of God. We go through our Christian lives asking, asking, asking. Only the unbounding generosity of the Creator prevents us from falling flat on our spiritual faces. Time and time again, God does give, freely, with no expectation from us.

Most Christians go through a Divine Uncle George phase at the beginning of their spiritual

10

journey. However, as they grow in knowledge and wisdom, they realize that this kind of asking/getting is spiritual milk rather than solid food (Heb. 5:11–14). For those who search for the meat and potatoes, Uncle George soon fades.

This same searching, however, leads Christians to discover the gifts that God *has* promised them. These are not the worldly "give-me's" of wealth and prosperity, but are the spiritual gifts that will equip us for a much more exciting, demanding life in the Spirit.

The giver of these enabling gifts is not a fly-by-night visitor in the guest room, but a permanent member of the family. And although this giver does not demand anything in return for these gifts, there is an expectation of more than a polite "thank-you" in response. Our expected response to these gifts is an affirmation that Jesus Christ is lord. Whether the response is in the form of believing or trusting, of risking or delighting, the gift is always ours to receive.

This kind of gift giving and affirmation response is the beginning of an exciting, dynamic relationship. Our heavenly Creator, not a Divine Uncle George, freely gives us these wonderful gifts. This is how I think of my Divine Uncle George—not a little known heavenly dispenser of worldly goods, but a loving parent who equips me to deal with my world. With great and glorious gifts like faith and strength and grace, powerful gifts such as victory over sin and power to the weak, humble gifts like my daily bread, and human gifts like rest, I can move ever onward and upward in my Christian walk, assured that whatever faces me, I have been given the resources to cope.

1

The Gift of Real Bread

"I am telling you the truth," Jesus said.
"What Moses gave you was not the bread from
heaven; it is my Father who gives you
the real bread from heaven."

—John 6:32

Sometimes, I have an inkling of how Jesus must have felt as he looked at the hungry five thousand. By the time I've finished feeding the gang at my house, I feel that the five thousand would have been a cinch. Jesus had five loaves, two fishes, and twelve helpers!

The first two gaping maws greet me at the door as I come home:

"What can we have for a snack?"

My brain lumbers from business into feeding gear. "An apple. Crackers and peanut butter. Two cookies. Any one of the above."

Before anything else, it's time to prepare the feed bucket for the chickens. I can never delay chicken food to a later, more convenient time since they begin to drift down the path from the barn at feeding time. Too much delay, and I have a yard full of flower-bed-destroying, lawn-scratching-up, vegetable-garden-marauding chickens. Not only are they insistent on a regular feeding schedule, but they also like a "hot mash" for supper, made with boiled potatoes and bran middlings. Add to this gooey mess anything scraped from the supper plates the night before and any leftover cereal, toast crusts, or bacon rinds from breakfast, and the chickens are in heaven.

The donkeys also like a regular feeding time. Tessa generally bellows across the barnyard when her stomach tells her that supper should be on its way. At least the donkeys are a little easier to feed: peelings from the supper vegetables, a few carrots, some bread slices, and an apple or two. They do, however, insist on a generous scoop of a commercial feed called "Horse Chunkies." I've learned the hard way not to let the supply run out. No horse chunkies and I'm chased out of the barn!

After Nathan has taken the donkey and chicken buckets up to the barn, I can turn my attention to the family's supper. Any working mother will agree that preparing supper at the end of a long business day is a refined form of modern torture. I've always planned to be prepared, but somehow I've never managed to "make-one, freeze-one" when lasagna is on the menu, or spent a happy Saturday cooking and freezing meals for the week ahead.

Instead, I'm always face-to-face with the five o'clock syndrome: "What to have for supper?" Like millions of others, I find something, do something with it, and serve it.

"Awwh. Chicken again?"

"Ugh! I hate liver!"

"Do I have to eat the meat loaf?"

"Didn't you make dessert?"

"Sorry, Honey, I had beef at lunch today."

"Did you put onions in this?"

"Can I have a hot dog instead?"

And that's not mentioning the times that:

I forgot to take the meat out of the freezer;

I took the meat out of the freezer, but the cat found it thawing on the counter and ate it;

the power went off with no warning during the crucial cooking hour;

the sauce for the spaghetti was all ready, and I discovered that there was no more spaghetti;

someone ate the leftover chicken I was saving for the chicken a la king.

After supper, as each member of the family goes off to various digestive activities, I still have seven cats that expect to be fed. Trying to open cans of cat food, pour out dry kibbles, fill bowls with water, and avoid stepping on or falling over a mewling, purring, ecstatic pussycat is a feat deserving of an Olympic gold medal.

Cats done, it's the dog's turn. He's no problem. He'll eat anything if I drizzle a little melted bacon fat over it.

Even after all this, feeding time is not yet over. The bird-feeders wait. Trudging out in rain, hail, sleet, or snow, I dutifully fill the swinging plastic containers with seed and suet. Not a moment too soon, the cheeky chickadees remind me.

I have just enough time to take a quick breather before the next round starts.

"What can I have for bedtime snack?"

"Anything to eat out there, Honey?"

"Can I have some more dessert?"

Small tokens are quickly dispensed. Then, the lunchboxes wait. I hate packing lunchboxes. Same old two sandwiches, three cookies, and an apple. They, too, are finally done. Feeding time at the zoo is over.

But the frightening thought is that it will all begin again tomorrow! Jesus obviously was just as exasperated when he saw the crowds that had followed him across Lake Galilee. The day before, he had performed the miracle of the loaves and fishes. From humble beginnings, he had made a meal that would eventually feed five thousand people. The next day, when the people looked for Jesus, they found him on the other side of the lake.

Sternly, he told them, "You are looking for me because you ate the bread and had all you wanted, not because you understood my miracles" (John 6:26). It seems that they were just looking for another free meal!

I can almost sense Jesus' exasperation as he goes on to tell them that he is the "bread of life" and that whoever eats this bread will never be hungry again. I wonder, though, whether this is what the crowd wanted to hear. There must have been a lot of hungry people, disappointed that they were being offered a spiritual bread when they were expecting something more physically substantial. So much of our time and energy is spent in securing the bread of this world for our tummies. So little is spent searching for the bread of life that Jesus offers.

We all know what it is like to feel hungry. First there is a minor discomfort. We usually take a moment or two to determine if this is a real hunger or if we are simply bored and feel like doing something, such as eating. If we are really hungry and ignore the first signals, our stomach sends up stronger messages: grumblings, rumblings, and embarrassing gurgles. If we continue to ignore these messages, our stomach moves into high gear: pain, cramping, and aches. Then the final stages: nausea, weakness, dizziness, palpitations, sweating—our whole body gets into the act. Anyone who has ever fasted knows all these symptoms. Anyone who has ever dieted knows every nuance of hunger pangs.

It's a shame that we don't feel the same kind of urgency when our spirits require feeding. The true bread of Jesus is always available to us, but we don't have the same overwhelming urges to gorge ourselves on its goodness. Instead, we take a nibble here and a nibble there when the going gets rough. A small crisis in our lives, and we look for the bread of life; a little storm in our otherwise placid seas, and we're ready to fill up on the bread of heaven. But, in our day-to-day lives, we're not hungry.

How much easier it would be if God had built some more identifiable hunger signals into our spirit: cramping, aching, nausea, dizziness! Instead, we must rely on a vague feeling of malaise, a hard-to-pinpoint unease, a fleeting flash that all isn't quite right. The hungry spirit is restless, yearning, but there are no physical symptoms to back it up.

The hungry spirit is also powerless. When we feel this powerlessness, when we know that we're not living triumphantly, then it is time for us to seek the true bread.

As with all of God's gifts, a responsive action is needed. In this case, we need only to believe in Jesus. In return, we receive the gift of true bread, which is eternal life.

Our spirit is fed. The restlessness is gone. In its place are the convictions that eternal life is ours and that Jesus is lord of our lives. My family keeps coming back for more food day after day, but once we have been fed the true bread, our spirits hunger no more.

2

The Gift of Faith

I assure you that if you have faith as big as a mustard seed, you can say to this hill, "Go from here to there!" and it will go.

—Matthew 17:20

One afternoon, I was having coffee with the ladies who work in the sewing room. I often like to stop in and chat while they create the beautiful costumes for the Pioneer Village where I work. During the course of the conversation, one of the ladies told me of the difficulty she had in trying to stop worrying about things. I said that not worrying was simply a matter of "letting go and letting God." Worrying suggested that the matter was too big for God to take care of and, therefore, that it required our intervention in the form of worrying.

"When I have a worrying situation," I told her, "every time I catch myself fussing over it, I apologize to God and consciously stop worrying about it any more. Even then I still want to remind God to solve my problem. Instead, however, I remind myself that God will take care of me, that I must trust God, and that worrying never helps solve a problem."

"I wish I had your faith!"

I've heard those words many times, and each time I feel a little niggle of guilt. Somehow, the speaker sees my apparent faith as a measure of my stature as a Christian. In many cases, the comment is not on my ability to use the gift of faith, but on my performance in a tough situation. There's a world of difference between the two.

Faith is a gift. It's not something that we can work up or practice or cultivate. It's not something that we have once in a while, only in some situations but not in others. It's not an exclusive gift only for the chosen few, and it's not an earned reward. It simply is.

The gift of faith is somewhat like having a million dollars in the bank. Great stuff, but only if you know it's there! Every Christian has the gift, but few know exactly how much they have in their account. Like the million dollars in the bank, how much of the gift we use depends entirely on how much of the gift we believe we have. It's a matter of trusting that God has given us enough "in the bank" to handle any emergency.

Whenever we come across a situation that we don't wish to change or hand over to the Lord for a solution, we often say that we just don't have that kind of faith—that the "money" simply isn't there to cover our "check."

Easy, and who can argue? I'm certainly in no position to judge the amount of faith that another Christian has . . . or am I? If I do a bit of research and check out *faith*, I find that it is another of God's free gifts to us.

One great passage in Hebrews, chapter 11, talks of faith in a bold and exciting way. In this chapter,

situation. There is a surety and certainty that, although I often can't see the work in my life right at the moment of turmoil, God is there.

Part of my problem, though, is that I always presume I need enough faith to handle the situation all at once. I remember when I was going through divorce proceedings. It was a terrible time for me, and if ever there is a time of testing for any human being, divorce must be the most stressful.

I was trying to handle the situation as best I could. Time and time again I would find myself worrying about it, and time and time again I would apologize to God and try to let the situation go. I knew that God would handle it, but I just couldn't get myself out of the picture. I was continually worrying about tomorrow or next week or next year. What would happen? Where would I go? Who would take care of us? I knew the answers to these questions were all in God's plan, but I just couldn't let go long enough to let it work out.

A good friend suggested to me that I try to handle only one day at a time instead of days or weeks or years. My faith might not stretch for forty-eight hours, but perhaps it could handle twenty-four. I tried it, but still I found I couldn't allow the Holy Spirit to give me peace and assurance.

Finally I realized that if my faith couldn't handle twenty-four hours, perhaps it could handle a smaller portion of time. I tried one-hour chunks. When I started to worry, especially late at night, I would look at the clock and tell the Lord that I wouldn't worry for the next hour. I had enough faith to believe that God could handle it all for an hour. On bad nghts, it would sometimes be five-minute chunks, but God honored my small portion of faith. For one hour, or for five minutes, the Almighty would give me the peace that comes with surrender, and I knew that for that space of time my faith would sustain me.

Perhaps that's why Christians talk about making a "leap of faith." A "leap of faith" is facing up to the impossible, trusting the Lord to help you through, and plunging into it on faith. But there is no law that says our "leaps" have to be giant ones. A small leap of a few feet can take just as much faith as a leap across a bottomless abyss. It all depends upon our point of view. I've always found the abyss leaps much easier than those little ones. Perhaps that's why people tend to admire what they perceive as my faith. What they are really seeing is my way of dealing with impossible situations.

When I took what looked like a "leap of faith," giving up a secure government job in Toronto and taking a short-term contract job in the wilds of eastern Ontario, other people thought I had really made a bold leap. Actually, it was a way of doing what I really wanted to do: I was tired of my Toronto job, I had always wanted to live in the country, and I was ready for a new career challenge. When the pieces started falling into place, I didn't find it difficult to believe that God would take care of my job security. After all, I *wanted* to believe it—the faith was easy.

And, as always, God did take care of me. My job became even more secure than the one I had left behind, and the move was easily the best thing that had happened in my life. When I talk about that move, my faith looks pretty good.

But don't ask me to talk about the smaller "steps"—the ones that I'm reluctant to take and would just as soon have an excuse to avoid completely. My faith doesn't easily seem to stretch that far. The small "leaps" often seem so much riskier than the large ones.

"Oh, I wish I had your faith." Not really. My faith is just as wavering and fragile as the next Christian's. However, as long as I can remember that my "bankbook" shows I have enough for any situation, I can cope—giant leaps or small steps, ten years or five minutes. Faith can cover it all.

3

The Gift of Eternal Life

*I give them eternal life, and they
shall never die. No one can
snatch them away from me.*
—John 10:28

When I went farm hunting, I prepared a shopping list of all the things it "must" have: lots of land, barn, fireplace, stream, pond, and apple trees. At first glance, Stillwater Farm came close to the ideal: lots of land, old barn, fireplace, small stream, two ponds, and surely, lots of apple trees in the back forty.

Once I had signed on the dotted line and began to look around, however, I made a few discoveries. The land was fine, but the barn needed some work ("some" is a euphemism for hours of backbreaking labor), the fireplace smoked continually, the stream dried up in mid-July, and ditto the two ponds. As for the back forty, a summer of searching turned up one small, miserable crab apple tree on the edge of the field.

I wasn't overly disappointed. One out of six wasn't bad, and I changed the score a little by planting a small orchard of apple trees. In ten or fifteen years, with the barn repaired and the trees bearing, the fireplace fixed and possibly the stream ditched, I would have it all.

Late in the fall of my first year at the farm, I went

for a long walk in the back pastures. Much of the heavy undergrowth was gone, and even the thick cedar bush had thinned out when the poplar and birch leaves darkened and fell. Walking along the edge of the dense green cedar, I suddenly noticed some bright red pieces in the deep green and brown mosaic of the bush wall. Intrigued, I pushed aside the outer fringe, and hidden behind a tall clump of cedars, I found an apple tree. Only the bright red of the apples on the topmost branches had given away its secret location.

I wondered how long it had been growing in the cedar bush, unnoticed by the passerby. The tree was tall, with a thick trunk and wide spreading branches. I put my hand on the gnarled, twisted trunk, feeling the rough bark, marbled with moss. Over the years, the apple tree had struggled, twisting and turning towards the elusive sunlight that the invading cedar had slowly closed out. I'm sure that the sun had not touched its lower limbs for many years—many were dead, leafless, and brittle to the touch. But on the very topmost branches, where the sun could still shine on the blossoms, small red fruit clustered. These were the bright flashes of color that had drawn me to the spot.

I decided that this was the apple tree on my list. Remembering the Bible verse, "By their fruits ye shall know them" (Matt. 7:20, KJV), I picked up one of the windfalls and took a bite. The apples were small and scabbed, but they were surprisingly sweet and delicious. This was my apple tree, all right.

On my next trip, I brought along a saw and spent several hours removing the cedar bushes along two sides of the apple tree. I also climbed the twisted, gnarled trunk and removed most of the dead limbs. All in all, I was quite proud of my handiwork.

More than that, I felt that I had found a priceless gift. There were no other trees nearby that could account for the presence of the lone apple tree. The apple was not one that I recognized as any of the popular garden varieties. Many years earlier, perhaps even before Stillwater Farm had been built, a stray apple seed had somehow found its way to the edge of the cedar bush and had taken a tenuous hold in the sandy soil. For years the tree had grown freely, until the cedar had slowly surrounded its trunk, eventually enclosing it in the dense undergrowth. Even so, the apple tree had continued to bear fruit. And even if the only benefactors were the birds and the small animals, the fruit had remained sweet and good.

What I had found was not just a wild tree, but a waiting gift of life.

One of the gifts that is promised to a Christian is the gift of eternal life. Somehow, it seems too big a gift for us to comprehend. We try to make it simple: "Pie in the sky when we die!" We think of eternal life as a "later" proposition: now I live, later I will experience eternal life. It is life after death rather than life after life. We make a separation between

31

living the Christian life and living the eternal life. The gift of eternal life seems to have no use to us here and now; it is simply a promise of some reward to come.

Since everything that I have learned about the Christian life has been concrete and down-to-earth, I find it difficult to accept eternal life as a spiritual gift of no earthly use now but of great worth after I die. I am convinced that every gift of God must have a purpose for us as we go about our daily lives—even the gift of eternal life.

Working on my old apple tree, pruning, shaping, watching it grow and flourish, I thought how well it symbolized the gift of eternal life. We are like the apple tree, planted in ground that may or may not be fertile, surrounded by the cedar bush of this world: sins, doubts, temptations, and sorrows. We twist and turn, always striving to reach the light, but because the gift of eternal life is within us, we continue to bear fruit here and now. Even when we feel stunted and cutoff, the fruit is there.

Eventually, of course, my old apple tree will die. I know, however, that it will continue to live in the seeds I have taken and carefully planted in my own garden.

Christians die, but their fruit also remains. The small seed of faith planted by their witness can grow into a mighty arm of God. So often, I've wondered about the person who originally brought the good news to some of the great evangelists, like Charles Wesley or Billy Graham. We never hear of them, and yet, without their fruit, so much of God's work might have been lost.

When I'm feeling that I have so little to give, that my Christian fountain has dried up, I remember the old apple tree. In the midst of the most adverse circumstances, it produced a sweet fruit. Within its broken and gnarled branches was the gift of life.

The gift of eternal life is within me, if I accept it. Trusting that Jesus is the Lord and Master of my life, knowing that the fruit I bear is his responsibility frees me from worrying about the cedar bush that sometimes seems to be closing in. I know, too, that when the time is right, it is God's hand that will free me from the bush, cutting away the branches and brambles that threaten my very existence.

When we accept the gift of eternal life, we know that although we are surrounded on all sides by this world, we are free: to grow, to produce fruit, and eventually, to pass from this life to yet another, more glorious life.

4

The Gift of the Kingdom

---

*Do not be afraid, little flock, for
your Father is pleased to give you
the Kingdom.*

—Luke 12:32

I am in the chicken business.

Sounds good, especially when I take a dozen brown eggs to my former colleagues in Toronto. They are impressed. They don't know that my "chicken business" consists of about thirty birds: one large, pompous rooster; one capon (mistakenly put in with laying hens instead of meat hens when he was a few days old); a dozen old laying hens; fourteen pullets (young hens not yet laying); and one chick.

They are more than just my business—they are family. Most of them have names. The rooster is called Victor, since he was the only one to survive in his clutch of three, and there's Friend, Medal, Blondie, and Doubtful. I have been through all the vicissitudes of life with them: births, deaths, disappointments (such as the time the old Broody Hen sat on her eggs through three long hot summer weeks and not one egg hatched!), and triumphs (two of the old girls raised the fourteen pullets between them).

I've worried about them in the cold winter months, carried kettles of hot water for their frozen bucket, mashed tons of hot potatoes for their favorite feed, and spent days winterizing their coop with yards of polyethylene sheeting.

I've fussed over them in the hot summer, making sure that they have a cooling breeze blowing through the coop, keeping their water fresh, and changing the straw daily in the laying boxes.

My chickens have a good life. In return, they supply me with lovely, large brown eggs. We all seem to think that it is an equitable arrangement.

Occasionally, however, our harmonious relationship is thrown off. Since they are allowed to roam around the barn and not kept in a pen, the hens need to be returned to the barn every night. Otherwise, they would be prey to every passing fox, dog, or bush wolf. Just at sunset, I bring them a bucket of their mash, call them in, and close the door.

Anyone who believes that chickens always "come home to roost" has never met my girls. They have a sixth sense that tells them when I am in a hurry and need to get away. That's the evening that they won't come in. I cajole, plead, threaten. It makes no difference. I know how silly I look, running around the barnyard chasing hens, but the only way to catch one is with a flying tackle. Even then I often end up with little more than a fistful of tail feathers for my effort. It's not one of my favorite times, and I usually return to the house swearing to get rid of the whole bunch of them.

When I added to my collection of cats, my

troubles with the chickens multiplied. The cats did not chase the chickens. Nothing so mundane. They found it much more rewarding to sit on the step of the chicken house at dusk and watch the silly chickens trying to get up enough nerve to come past them to get in. They would lurk in a dark corner of the coop, wait until all were safely gathered in, and leap out at an imaginary mouse. All thirty-plus birds would go into full-flapping confusion and it would be some time before I could get them settled again. Sunset was becoming a time of unrest and riot at the chicken house.

One evening, as I drove in the driveway, Nathan met me with the news that the chickens were missing.

"All of them?" I asked incredulously.

"Most of them," said Nathan. "There's only a few pullets and one or two old hens left. I don't know what happened to them."

I had visions of a stray dog or a marauding fox on the loose during the day, but my neighbors assured me that they had seen nothing. I knew, too, that the donkeys in the paddock usually took care of any curious canines in the vicinity.

I was upset, worried that my poor "chickies" had met with some terrible fate. (In my deepest heart, though, there was a small sigh of relief: only fifteen of the silly birds left to worry about.)

At sunset I made up the usual bucket of mash and started out. Usually, the chickens ran down the pathway and met me halfway, getting underfoot and generally making it well-nigh impossible to move. Tonight, however, only one chicken was on the path, and when she saw me, she rushed off clucking into the thick undergrowth. I couldn't think what would upset her so much that she would ignore her food.

I saw other chickens lurking in the undergrowth and found several more cowering in the barn. Two or three were hiding in the nesting boxes, and the remaining hens were scattered across the paddock. None of them would come near the chicken coop.

As I reached the coop, I saw one hen pressed against the side of the barn. She seemed prostrate with fear. I put down the bucket and went over to her. Suddenly she exploded into action! As she leapt up into the air, wings flapping and feathers flying, I saw that her foot was tangled in the handle of a white plastic grocery bag. As she ran from the white menace behind her, it filled with air and became a fluttering, crackling, moving "thing." The other chickens, seeing the hen with the "thing" coming towards them, ran off in every possible direction.

The poor lady with the grocery bag finally came up against the far wall of the coop. She pressed herself into a corner and cowered, dumb with fright. Gently, I lifted her up and took the bag off her leg. Then began the long process of reassuring all the other hens. Gentle cluckings, soft words, the promise of warm mash, and eventually they all "came home to roost."

I wonder if Jesus was thinking about chickens like mine when he used them as a way of describing us. In Luke 12:32, he says, "Do not be afraid, little flock, for your Father is pleased to give you the Kingdom." Some may think that he was referring to a flock of sheep, but I am convinced that he meant chickens. He used the same idea another time when he talked about gathering the people to him "as a hen gathers her chicks under her wings" (Luke 13:34). I think Jesus knew chickens and could see how very similar we are to them in terms of our spiritual strivings.

My chicken with the plastic bag is a perfect picture of how we can be completely paralyzed by our fears. We fear for our belongings, our families, our livelihood. We fear for our survival in this world, for the future of our children, for the means to meet next month's mortgage payment. We fear for our health, for our mental stability, for our emotional happiness. We fear death, taxes, and the dentist. No wonder we spend our lives cowering in the corner, unable to move. And when we do gather up enough courage to make a move, no matter how small, our fears blow themselves up out of proportion and chase us into an even greater state of immobility. Our fears become so great that they affect those around us. Soon our family, our friends, even our co-workers run from us and our mounting fears.

If you've ever spent time with pessimistic people; those who see darkness, gloom, and destruction in everything; those who always point out how it will all go wrong; those who list their fears one by one, you know how depressing it can be. Eventually, you dread being with those people altogether. In fact, you try to avoid them if at all possible. If we're not careful, our fears can turn us into "those people."

Jesus sees us and how our fears bind us. He finds us cowering against the fence, unable to move, terrified. Gently, he releases us and tells us, "Fear not." And then he goes on to tell us of a promised gift: the kingdom.

If you read the next few verses of the Luke 12 passage, Jesus tells us more about this gift we will receive. It is the kingdom where there is no decay, where the moth cannot destroy, where all we have is safe forever. It is a haven, a resting place, a refuge created especially for us.

When I find that my fears are getting the better of me and I am spending a lot of time in worry and doubt, I try to remember the chicken and the plastic bag. My fears are just about as substantial as hers were—no more than a bagful of wind. And I know, when I finally work myself into a state of complete paralysis, the gentle hand of Jesus is always waiting, ready to free me and offer me the gift of the kingdom, where plastic bag fears are reduced to nothing.

5

The Gift of Grace

*But by the free gift of God's grace
all are put right with him through
Christ Jesus, who sets them free.*

—Romans 3:24

One evening, during a "talk-it-over" session, a group of Christian friends began to share the stories of how they had found the Christian life and what had led to their conversion. These stories were honest and personal. Such was the feeling of security within the group that I felt free to share some of my own early story.

It isn't a story that is particularly dramatic, nor is it particularly sordid. I hadn't committed any really terrific sins, but only the usual kind, with a few personal touches thrown in. I hadn't come back from the edge of alcoholism; I hadn't been rescued from a life of crime; I hadn't even been a destitute, prostitute, or profligate. In short, I think it is a pretty average story—a few highlights here and there, but nothing that would make for a startling exposé.

When I finished, there was a collective sigh around the room. One lady, who had been particularly attentive, said that my story gave her hope for her erring daughter. I began to feel a trifle uncomfortable—I didn't like being cast in the "prodigal daughter" mold. But I smiled anyway and commented how wonderful it was that the Lord can use our experiences to benefit other Christians.

Unfortunately, I wasn't so easily let off the hook. Another member of the group, one who had been very quiet all evening, turned to me and said, "Isn't the Lord gracious and good? I think at this point, it would be appropriate for us to sing 'Amazing Grace.' Somehow, it seems to point up the grace of God at work in Pat's life."

> Amazing grace! how sweet the sound
> That saved a wretch like me!

And they all began to sing. Except me. I didn't like to think that a sinner's song such as "Amazing Grace" applied to me.

Grace seemed so much bigger than my small sins of errors and omission. Grace was meant for the big fish—the larger-than-life sinners such as the author of this hymn. He was a man who had been a slave trader, a drunkard, and in every way exhibited the bestiality in humanity. Grace is for the woman at the well who met Jesus and was told to go and sin no more—she was a natural recipient. But for people like me, small *s* sinners, grace was surely too big a gift to bestow. A little forgiveness, perhaps, but *grace*?

From that evening on, I began to think about grace as one of God's gifts that *was* meant for me, not just the capital *s* Sinners. I decided to embark on a little biblical research. For most people, this would mean an in-depth search, but I am a very "now! right away!" person. My "research" consisted of two phases: (1) get out the concordance and look up the word *grace*, and (2) get out the Bible and look up all the references I found in the concordance.

It didn't take long to find the answers to the two questions that had been worrying me. I now know who receives grace and how they receive it. The answers are that everyone can receive grace (even me) by a free gift from God. But there had to be more to it than that. How could something so theologically puzzling be so simple?

According to one of my references, Ephesians 2:1-10, everyone has at one time or another lived a worldly life following their own desires. Whether these desires create big sins or small sins makes no difference. Because of this sinful state, everyone is eligible to receive grace. Grace is the way or the means by which a person is saved.

This passage also reveals that I can't earn grace: it is a free gift. Neither can I deserve more or less grace: the size of my sins makes no difference. The grace that I receive is just as large as the grace offered to a murderer or drug addict. A sobering thought, to say the least. Does that mean that God sees all sins as equal? Does God love each of us equally, regardless of our sin? Or is grace simply a free gift, available to all, the only criteria being our willingness to accept it?

This passage from Ephesians also tells me that I can't boast about having received grace. It doesn't make me a bigger, better, or bolder person. It simply makes me a saved Christian.

From Ephesians, I dipped into James and found a verse, which James borrowed from Proverbs, that struck home. "God resists the proud, but gives grace to the humble" (James 4:6). Humble? Not me. At least, not often me. What kind of humble does God require?

This is where I left my search. The answers were there, but I couldn't see how they applied to my life or how the gift of grace could possibly be for me. The answers I *had* found certainly hadn't made me feel any better about being the subject of "Amazing Grace." If anything, I was more confused than ever. Typical of my way of dealing with confusing issues, I promptly put it away and forgot about it. Twelve years later, Maggie showed me the truth behind God's grace.

Maggie is an old gray donkey. No one really knows how old she is. Since donkeys can live for forty-five years, she could be anywhere between twenty and forty. That's old for a donkey.

I first saw Maggie at a "donkey farm." The family had seen the farm in a magazine, in a small advertisement offering donkeys for sale. I had never seen a real donkey and had certainly never thought about owning one. But here we were with one hundred acres and nothing eating it. The thought of buying a donkey wasn't exactly outside

45

the bounds of possibility anymore. I called the farm and had a long chat with a most exuberant lady who was definitely a "donkey person." By the time I hung up, I was committed to a visit, even though the prices she quoted were a little daunting.

We went to the farm on a cold, wet, rainy March day. The drive was long and tedious. Several times we were lost on the circuitous country lanes that Val had described to me. However, just as she promised, we eventually found the farm that had several male donkeys pegged out front. As we turned into the driveway, loud brays announced our arrival. (If you have never heard a donkey bray, which I hadn't, it sounds like an elephant clearing its throat of a particularly nasty piece of hay—I think. Sufficient to say, the sound is loud, rough, and echoing.)

Val came out to greet us, and, before we could catch our breath, we were standing in a paddock filled with donkeys. The donkeys crowded around us, nuzzling our clothes and breathing down our necks. At first, I was, quite frankly, terrified. Donkeys aren't as large as horses, but they are a lot larger than a dog. I had visions of a donkey stampede with me underneath. It soon became obvious, however, that these were gentle, curious creatures. Eagerly, they took the bread slices that Val had brought for us to feed them. The bolder ones poked their noses into our pockets looking for

46

more. One small donkey leaned lovingly against my side, and another held its head forward for me to scratch behind the long ears. They were all enchanting. Soft brown muzzles, silky ears, small delicate hooves, intelligent eyes fringed with incredibly long lashes. Many had the dark cross marking on their back, traditionally said to be a sign that their ancestor carried Jesus into Jerusalem.

We were sold. We had to have one. One small brown donkey followed my mother everywhere she went, so we chose Alexis. Unfortunately, Alexis was still a young donkey and hadn't been broken for riding. We wanted Alexis, but we also wanted a donkey that the children could ride.

Val had a solution: buy two. Donkeys are happier if they have a companion, she told us, and the two donkeys would keep each other company. Of course, she also reminded us, broken donkeys cost more.

Of course.

Then she made a suggestion. She did have one donkey that might interest us, a dapple-gray that she had bought only a month before in a consignment from the States. She didn't know very much about the donkey, except that she was very gentle and was broken both for riding and for pulling. She had belonged to several owners, one of whom had used her for all his farm work. She was of uncertain age, but Val thought she might be

47

twelve or thirteen years old. She had been sold just the week before, but when the new owners saw her, they had canceled the sale.

No wonder. Poor Maggie. Not a beautiful animal at best, she was heavier than the other donkeys around her. Her shoulders were wider; and, instead of the small delicate black hooves, she had broad, wide feet and heavy legs. Her head was broad, too, and she had a pendulous underlip that gave her a petulant expression. But worst of all, she had suffered from some kind of reaction to Val's liberal dusting of flea powder. Most of the hair on her back had fallen out, leaving great patches of black skin. Even as I rubbed my hand across her back, hanks of hair came away. Combining these qualities with her general air of dejection and disinterest, she was not an appealing sight.

We all tried to hide our dismay. After the field full of lively brown donkeys, Maggie was a sorry contrast. However, we let Val put a saddle and bridle on her and noted how the donkey stood still and allowed Cherith to mount. Down the driveway they went, Maggie plodding along, looking neither left nor right, going not one pace faster than necessary. Back they came, and Nathan climbed aboard. Maggie didn't even glance up at the change of passengers. I gingerly rubbed my hand behind her ears. She didn't react. Maggie was making it abundantly clear that she couldn't care less. Whatever her past had been, it had not given her any hope for a future that could be better.

Something in her humble manner appealed to us, and we decided to buy Maggie. (As you may have guessed, she was a bargain price!) Impulsively, I took her head in my hands and pulled it up so that she and I were eye-to-eye.

"I'm taking you home, Maggie," I said. "To a wonderful place where you'll have green fields to roam, fresh hay, and a warm barn in the winter." Maggie simply looked at me.

Three weeks later, Maggie and Alexis arrived. Alexis bounded around the acres of fields that were hers, examined every inch of the barn, and enthusiastically devoured the pile of fresh hay. Maggie simply stood in the paddock and looked around. It was days before she began to believe the promise I had made her.

Now, two years later, Maggie is at home. She enjoys her fields, the warm barn, the fresh hay. Most of all, she enjoys the company of the children, loves visitors, and always looks for a snack.

Maggie is enjoying my gift of grace. When I see Maggie standing under the shade of the crab apple tree dozing in the afternoon sun, or when she nuzzles her head under my arm so that I can tickle her chin, I see the result of "grace to the humble." Maggie didn't ask to be saved from the donkey farm; she probably didn't feel that she deserved to be saved. Maggie simply accepted the free gift, and from that time on, enjoyed its benefits.

That's how grace works. We don't need to ask for grace; we don't need to convince the Lord that we deserve it. We simply accept it, through faith, and then enjoy the results.

And the results for us? A wonderful freedom! Like Maggie's large fields, the world is now ours, with no restrictions, while we are walking in the spirit. The daily bread is always there for us to savor, and we need never again take thought for the morrow. Like Maggie, we can simply bask in the warm sunshine of God's grace.

Since meeting Maggie, I can sing "Amazing Grace" with complete confidence that the story is mine also. I too "once was lost, but now am found, was blind, but now I see."

6

The Gift of Wisdom

---

*If any of you lacks wisdom, he should
pray to God, who will give it to him; because
God gives generously and graciously to all.*

—James 1:5

"I have just cut off my thumb!"

Pink Panther movie devotees will remember that phrase from one memorable scene in which Clouseau's boss has a nasty accident with his toy guillotine. It was a favorite warning of my family whenever a sharp knife was wielded on the family meat or the resident hairstylist was working on some hapless head. It was a phrase used in jest to point up the perils of being near when I had a sharp instrument in my hand. I have numerous minor scars as witness to my lack of skill in the cutting, sawing, chopping, hacking, or snipping fields. In fact, all four of the fingers on my left hand bear the hallmark of the nearsighted.

Realizing my shortcomings, I have become more careful in my use of any sharp instrument. In fact, I verge on paranoia when slicing meat or frozen bread or a waxed turnip. I have learned the fine art of defense: always wear an oven mitt on the left hand and never, never slice without checking the whereabouts of all fingers and thumbs. The result of this caution has been an accident-free record for over ten years.

At Stillwater Farm, I discovered a whole new area of sharp-edged instruments. Chopping wood for the fire was not just an opportunity to exercise, it was a necessity for winter comfort. I bought a good, not large but very sharp ax.

One look at its edge left me in no doubt that my accident-free record might be in jeopardy. If anything, I would have to practice even more caution. I bought a pair of heavy work boots, and although I am famous for my penchant for working barefoot, I never picked up the ax without those boots on.

I found a soft piece of ground and a large piece of wood for a base, and I learned to chop with the wood resting on the base, my feet spread wide. If I missed the wood, the ax landed safely in the ground or into the wooden base. I became quite adept at chopping wood into manageable pieces for the fire, and I must admit, there is a certain excitement associated with the gradual growth of a pile of chopped firewood.

I soon felt confident enough to graduate to kindling, which is another thing altogether. This is taking one of the chopped pieces of wood and splitting it into thin strips which can easily be used to start a fire. The difficulty lies in the small slice of wood that must be split off. The ax blade must land precisely on the grain edge of the wood to take off a nice, thin slice.

One afternoon, I had an hour or two before I was to go out to an evening business function, and I decided to chop some kindling. It was a golden autumn day, and I was really enjoying the growth of my kindling pile. I felt like the perfect pioneer woman preparing her homestead for the long winter to come. In fact, I was doing so well, I decided to hold the kindling steady with one hand while I gently guided the ax with the other—real woodsman style. It was working wonderfully. At last, I had some control over the wood, and I realized that as long as I watched the ax, my left hand, and the top edge of the wood, I could easily chop off exactly the piece of kindling I wanted.

Concentration was the key.

I still don't know what happened. I have a vague memory of hearing the television antenna turning on the roof, seeing a skein of geese fly overhead in the corner of my eye, and hearing Nathan call out to me. Whatever the distraction was, the inevitable happened.

"I have just cut off my thumb!"

Well, not quite, but as near as possible. I cut off the top of it through the nail. I'll save the gory details—I'm sure that many are as squeamish about these things as I am. Suffice to say, it needed more than a Band-Aid and a kiss.

The hospital was nearly twenty miles away, and I knew I wouldn't be able to drive, since I was holding my left thumb together with a thick towel. I called my nearest neighbors, but their daughter told me her parents were out. However, her grandfather was home, and he had a car.

"Could he come right away?" I asked.

"I'll send him right down," she assured me.

Ten long minutes later, he arrived, walking.

"Where's your car?" I asked, trying to keep the strain out of my voice.

"Oh," he said. "I thought I'd like to try to drive yours." The neighbors had all been very interested in the arrival of my Renault Le Car, the first of its kind in the area. No doubt he saw this as the perfect opportunity to try it out.

This wasn't a time to argue. "OK, here's the keys." We got in.

"Haven't driven a standard shift in years," he said. "Where's the clutch?" Immediately, I knew I was in trouble. Tensely, I gave him a quick run down on the clutch position and gears.

Five minutes later, he was still struggling to find reverse gear. Reverse on the Le Car requires pushing down and then pushing over and back. Eventually, I did it for him using my good hand, while still holding the towel around my left. He immediately popped the clutch and stalled the car. We started again. This time, the car lurched backward. Fortunately we weren't going too fast, because he drove directly into one of the big trees on the lawn.

Somehow, we got down the lane and onto the main road. Only nineteen and three-quarters more miles to go! And all of it was on a four-lane transcontinental superhighway.

"We should be there in about twenty minutes," I

said, wondering if I had enough blood supply to last that long.

"I think we'll take the back road," he said. "I'm not too used to this car, and I don't care to drive it on the highway."

That turned out to be a wise suggestion. He was uncomfortable with my direct front-wheel drive steering as well, and we meandered back and forth over the middle line and occasionally onto the shoulder. After the initial grinding and squealing of my gears, I suggested that I do the shifting. All he had to do was let the clutch out and steer.

Somewhere after the first five miles, we lost third gear. I don't know how—it just wasn't there. By this time, I was in no condition to fiddle around looking for it. I just shifted directly from second to fourth and said a prayer for the transmission. I also prayed that we wouldn't have to use reverse again.

Forty minutes later, we arrived at the emergency entrance to the hospital. My neighbor let me off and said he'd park the car and be right back. I bid a mental farewell to Le Car.

Inside, I didn't have a chance to say a word before I was hustled onto a stretcher, with a warm blanket wrapped around me.

"You're in shock," said the nurse.

"Not from my injury," I told her, "but from the last twenty miles."

Eventually, they sewed the top of my thumb back on, filled me full of antibiotics and tetanus, and told me I could go.

I drove home—don't ask how. I just know it was a lot easier with my thumb immobilized in a splint than it had been when I was holding it on with a towel.

I didn't find third gear. In fact, I never found it again. Eventually, I took my car to a garage, where the mechanic told me that the "bushing" had gone and wondered how I had managed to do that. I didn't think he wanted to know, so I just looked noncommittal and paid the bill.

Now I have evidence on all five digits of my left hand to remind me that I cannot let my guard down when I am using a sharp-edged instrument of any kind. I also have a reminder that all the knowledge in the world cannot help me if I do not have the wisdom to use it. I knew that I could injure myself with the ax. I knew that my past experience showed the danger of using sharp tools. I knew that I was taking a chance by holding the wood with my unprotected hand. I knew that a split second of inattention could spell disaster.

Yet I went ahead and did it anyway. The knowledge was there, but the wisdom, which would have provided insight and understanding, was lacking. With wisdom I would have put the knowledge and experience I have gained to use. Wisdom would have made me more prudent. It would have brought a sense of reason to what I already knew.

Human wisdom is such a nebulous concept. We are wise sometimes and foolish others. "If only I knew then what I know now," we cry, thinking that our present knowledge could save us from our past mistakes. Not likely. What we needed then was not knowledge, but wisdom.

Paul says that human wisdom is foolish in God's eyes, but I've often thought that the reverse is true as well. So often, the wisdom of God looks foolish in the eyes of people.

I'm sure that a suburban minister who leaves a comfortable church to minister in some poverty-stricken missionary station is seen as foolish by those more "practical-minded" Christians.

"Why would you want to leave all this and go there?" they ask. "You don't know a thing about being a missionary."

It's not knowledge that is always needed—my scarred thumb silently testifies to the woeful inadequacy of human knowledge. Only divine wisdom can use this human knowledge to lead us along new pathways with the assurance that the resources will be provided to cope with the challenges of the road ahead.

As Christians, we are occasionally called to leave the safe parameters of our world to step into situations for which we may not always feel adequate. Our Christian motivation may be suspect by the wisdom of this world, which often calls instead for personal advancement and material gain. Those Christians who comfort the terminally ill, visit criminals, work with troubled teens, or counsel alcoholics and drug addicts cannot always give a reason for their commitment to those who are "worldly wise." Yet they know that the wisdom of God, given to them as a gift to bolster their human knowledge, helps them cope with any situation that may arise.

As for you and me, we also may face skepticism when we go beyond our normal church involvement and set off on a new adventure in our spiritual journey.

"Is that wise?" we might be asked, even by fellow Christians.

"No," we must answer, "not by the measure of this world." But in the world of the spirit, which we can glimpse with the gift of wisdom, it may be among the wisest things we will ever do.

7

The Gift of Healing

One and the same Spirit gives faith to one person, while to another person he gives the power to heal.

—1 Corinthians 12:9

Whenever someone asks me if I have had any firsthand experience with the gift of healing, I always hesitate. Not because I don't believe in healing, and not because I've never experienced healing, but because I know the angels in heaven chuckle every time I tell my story.

Other Christians recount tremendous testimonies of healing: bones have knit, tumors have disappeared, and senses have been restored. But not once have I met someone else with a miracle like mine. That is not to say that my experience of healing is less real—it's just a little less dramatic. It is also an account of my own self-centeredness, when I'd prefer to call it an account of my selfless concern for others.

I was working as a church secretary, and much to my joy and sometimes dismay, the pastor, Bernie Warren, occasionally invited me to join him in prayer for those he counseled.

One afternoon, Bernie called me into the church, where he was praying for a young woman with an eye problem. She was kneeling at the altar, and he was standing on one side of her with his hand on her head. He motioned for me to take my place on her other side. Gingerly, for I was relatively new to this prayer business, I laid my hand on her head and began to pray.

As I stood there, I became more and more conscious of pain emanating from my foot. I had a badly ingrown toenail, and because I had already undergone surgery for a similar problem on the other foot, I had tenderly been nursing this one along. I stood as little as possible, rode instead of walked, and took my shoes off at every opportunity. Standing there in the church, with my shoes on, increased pressure on the sensitive toe. Soon my mind was full of nothing but the pain in my toe and how much I wanted to sit down and take my shoe off.

Finally, I sent a mental note to the Lord: "If you want me to pray for this lady, you're going to have to fix my toe."

This seemed to clear my mind, because I was then able to get down to the serious business of praying for the woman's eyes.

I didn't realize until I started back to my office that my toe was no longer throbbing. Back at my desk, I took my shoe off. My toe looked better! With increasing disbelief, I took off my stockings and looked closely at the offending toe. The swelling was gone. It was no longer red and inflamed! Carefully, I squeezed the nail edge. Instead of the usual spurt of excruciating pain, I felt only the gentle pressure of my fingers. Boldly, I kicked the desk drawer. This should have sent me through the ceiling, but no pain resulted.

"Hey, Bernie," I yelled down the corridor, "guess what? God did it. My toe is better!"

I have to admit that I don't even know what finally happened with the woman's eyes, but I do know that my toe was healed that afternoon. My healing may not have the miraculous ring of healing some terrifying disease, but every time I look at my toe and compare it with the toe that was surgically repaired, I can see the exciting evidence of the healing power of God in my life.

It is this right-on-the-end-of-my-foot evidence that gives me the confidence to ask for the gift of healing for others. I know that it works, and I have found that people are much more receptive to the miracle of healing when they can see that God cares enough to heal the little agonies as well as the all-encompassing ones.

Occasionally God bestows the gift of healing on me without my asking for it. At these times, it is just as overwhelming a joy.

When Nathan was three years old, he caught his hand in the aluminum screen door just as we were going out. He had rested his hand between the rigid screen frame and the door jamb. When the door closed, his hand was caught, and it was several seconds before anyone could carefully open the screen again.

One look at the hand, and I knew it was serious. The fingers were badly squashed, and as I looked, the whole hand began to turn purple. Nathan was in agony. I didn't stop to think. I just took his hand between mine and started to pray. All I wanted to do was ease his pain.

"Jesus will fix it, Nathan," I told him. I prayed out loud so that Nathan could hear what I was saying and respond to the words. Within minutes, he stopped crying. I continued to hold his hand and pray. Nathan soon told me that it didn't hurt anymore, and that I could let go. The hand was completely healed! No swelling, no squash, and no discoloration. Nathan wasn't surprised, but I was. Even though I prayed for healing, I would have been satisfied with just an easing of the pain, but Jesus is never satisfied with less than a complete job.

Both my toe and Nathan's hand are examples of spontaneous healings. In neither case did I contemplate the possibility of healing taking place, but I also did not limit my expectations. I simply reacted to the situation with prayer.

On the few occasions when I've been asked to specifically pray for a healing for someone, I've had varied experiences. Unlike my spontaneous prayers for healing, I feel a need to get into the will of God before I can pray for the healing to take place. I also need to have some sort of compassion or empathy with the person. I can remember a friend asking me to pray for her son, who had cancer. This seemed a perfect kind of situation for healing to take place. The boy was young; the mother desperate. But there were a number of peripheral considerations that would need to be sorted out first.

The mother had been a strong Christian in her youth, but, for her own private reasons, had left the church and the Lord far behind her. Only in agony over her son did she cry out to the Lord.

The son was a rambunctious, aggressive, bullying kind of boy. Honesty forces me to admit that I never really liked him a whole lot. Many times I had reacted negatively to his rude manner, and now I needed to feel compassion for him.

It was a difficult situation, but I promised the mother that I would pray for the boy. Unfortunately, no matter how many times I tried to pray for a healing, my feelings toward the boy and his mother got in the way. I could only see him as a brat and her as a lapsed Christian. Not a conducive atmosphere for prayer. I finally realized that I was not the one to be praying. I called several of my Christian friends and, without telling them of the personalities of the two, asked them to pray for a sixteen-year-old boy with cancer and for his mother, who was trying to reach out to God in the situation. This was a scenario that instantly sparked compassion in my friends. They made the boy a prayer priority at their groups and started a prayer chain for him. One member felt called to fast for the situation.

After two years, although there was no spontaneous healing such as Nathan's hand, the boy continues to live, long after the doctors had declared he had only a short time left. The healing is in process, and whether it will eventually be a healing of the physical body, or a healing of the spiritual being, I don't know.

It is only recently that I have discovered healing of the spiritual being, or "healing of the memories." I'm sure everyone knows of some memory from childhood or later that continues to haunt them. I certainly had mine.

When I was twelve years old, my arch rival, Judy Kobelko, had a birthday party and invited everyone in the class but me. I was desperately hurt. I couldn't believe anyone could be so mean, and I even asked her if she had made a mistake. I often think what a triumph it must have been for her to tell me to my face that she didn't want me at her party.

The memory of that rejection rankled for many years, and Judy and I continued to be rivals through high school. She was a cheerleader, very pretty and popular, and I in turn was on the school council and very active in the drama club. When she finally dropped out in eleventh grade to get married, I secretly heaved a sigh of relief.

Years later, I discovered that the birthday-party rejection still had a hold over me. I would often feel that people were leaving me out, deliberately not including me in their plans. Secretly, I suspected that they didn't want me. If a group had a meeting and I wasn't invited, it hurt. Even if it was a group I didn't want to attend, I wanted to be invited. Soon, I started to refuse all invitations—"they're only asking me because they have to," I reasoned.

A good friend saw what was happening and suggested that we pray about it. In the course of prayer, the memory of Judy's party came to me. My friend prayed for the healing of this memory, asking Jesus to go back to that moment and, where I had felt hurt, to heal.

It worked. Here I am, writing about that birthday party with no residual bitterness. I can honestly say that I don't resent it when, for whatever reason, I am not asked to be involved in a group or meeting. My inner spiritual healing has taken place.

God's gift of healing is probably the most exciting gift of all the gifts offered. Not just because we can see physical evidence of the gift, but because there are levels of healing that we can only begin to guess at. When we pray for a physical healing, we must realize that healing of a far more complex nature is actually taking place.

If someone tells me that they prayed for a physical healing and nothing happened, I always suggest that they look for the answered prayer on another level. The spirit of God can see where the healing is needed. Where the world sees only physical needs, the spirit can see inner needs. God responds to the need, whether physical, emotional, or spiritual, with the most effective healing that can occur, bringing the person to the state where he can glorify God. For me to suggest that healing "didn't work" is to presume that I know better than my Lord what healing needs to be done.

Although we have many recorded stories of Jesus physically healing people, the New Testament records only three others who had the gift of physical healing: Peter, who healed the man at the temple gate; Phillip, who preached and healed in Samaria; and Paul, who healed Publius's father. Does this mean that no one else ever prayed for healing? I doubt it. Instead, it probably illustrates that healing takes place in many forms.

In First Corinthians 12:9, the King James Version of the Bible translates this spiritual gift as the "gifts of healing." The plural use of gift does not mean that there are many *gifts* of healing, but that there are many *kinds* of healing. God wants to heal the whole being: physically, emotionally, mentally, and spiritually. These gifts of healing allow just that to happen.

As Christians, we should seek to understand and accept the gifts of healing. In a world of hurting people, we must take some responsibility for helping them to heal. However, our Lord graciously allows us to leave the responsibility of the kind of healing to heavenly discernment. Our role is prayer: God can and will heal.

After all—I have a toe that tells the world of God's healing power.

8

The Gift of the Desires of Your Heart

*Take delight in the Lord, and he will
give you the desires of your heart.*
—Psalm 37:4, RSV

New Year's Day has always had special significance to me. It is a day of new beginnings, new resolutions, and new joys.

I remember many memorable New Year's Days:

the New Year's Day we discovered a city park full of hungry ducks and began a whole new winter tradition;

the New Year's Day the congregation of the small Newfoundland outport came to call, and we knew we were finally accepted by them;

the New Year's Day we walked around the back woods of Stillwater Farm and left jelly beans for the animals.

And I remember last New Year's Day, when the owl came. At first, we thought he was something caught on the top of the clothesline pole. Except for his feathers ruffling slightly in the cold wind, he was motionless.

"What's that?" asked Cherith.

"Looks like a piece of cloth has gotten blown around the pole," I replied.

We ignored it until it was time for Nathan to go to

the barn and do his chores. Seconds later he was back in. "That's an owl on the pole!" he exclaimed.

"Don't be silly," my sweet voice of adult reason replied. "It's broad daylight, and no owl is that big."

"Yes it is. He turned his head and watched me. It's an owl."

"Get the binoculars," I told him. Not that they were of any great use since one lens was missing, but you could see something if you squinted with one eye through the good lens.

"It is an owl!" An unbelievably big, brownish gray owl. "Get the bird book and we'll see what kind he is."

At that moment, the phone rang. It was a man who my friends had insisted would be "just perfect" for me. I'd forgotten that he was supposed to call and make a date. (I'd also forgotten what a date was, so I had been looking forward to this phone meeting.) I decided that the fact he was calling on New Year's Day was very auspicious.

After very hasty preliminaries, I told him, "We've got an owl in the yard. A large one. Nathan's looking him up now in the bird book." It was hard to talk balancing the telephone, binoculars, and bird book.

"That's nice," he said and changed the subject to something like favorite restaurants, hobbies, and horoscope signs. I wasn't really listening. I was trying to squint through the binoculars and compare the owl to the pictures in the book.

71

"He's not moving at all. Just sitting on the post. Wait! He just turned his head. He's looking right at us."

The man expressed polite interest and pressed on with his exploration of our mutual friends, interests, and philosophies.

"It's a great gray owl. There's a picture of him right here in the book. Yup. It's a great gray, all right. I wonder what he's doing around here?"

The man allowed that the owl was probably lost and went on to ask me about my job and career plans.

"Cherith's going outside to see how close she can get to him. He's so big, he's kind of scary. I hope he won't eat the chickens."

There was no reply. Obviously, I had finally caught his attention.

"No, they're safe. Says right here in the book that great grays don't go after domestic birds. Gosh! Cherith's really close to him. He doesn't seem frightened at all."

Cherith had gotten within a few feet of the bird. Mentally, I measured him against her height.

"He's nearly two feet high. I wonder if I should call the local bird-watcher's group or the naturalist society or something."

"I thought we might go out this afternoon. Perhaps for a drive along the river and then out for supper somewhere." My man was still there.

"This afternoon? But I have an owl, a great gray owl, in the yard. Why don't you come over here, meet the family, stay awhile, and watch the owl with us?"

"Hmmm . . ." His voice noticeably lacked enthusiasm. "Suppose we skip the owl and just go somewhere? That would give us an opportunity to become better acquainted."

"Skip the owl! This isn't just any owl—he's very rare. I may never see a great gray owl again. It says right here that they live in the Arctic and never come south unless the food is scarce."

He started to say something, but I interrupted.

"Hold it! He's moving! He's flying to the other side of the house. Hang on for a moment. I'll be right back." I dropped the phone and sped to the back window, just in time to see the owl effortlessly swoop across the lawn and land in the maple tree.

"Quick! Upstairs! I bet we can see him from Granny's window." We all pounded up the stairs to Mother's room and pressed our noses against the pane. There was the owl, literally feet away. Again, he showed no fear, merely returning our stares.

Suddenly, he spread his great wings and flew back toward the front of the house. We galloped from window to window, calling to each other as we spied him.

"He's in the cedar tree. Come and see."

"Oh, look, he's going toward the barn."

"Here he is. Here he is. He's back on the clothesline pole."

"Go and get me the binoculars. They're by the phone."

"Mommy, who left the phone off the hook? There's no one there." Click.

So much for the auspicious day of new beginnings. The man did not call back again, and I can only console myself with the thought that a man who couldn't get excited over a great gray owl probably wouldn't be compatible with someone who did.

The owl stayed at Stillwater Farm for several days. We became accustomed to his presence on the clothesline pole or in the cedar tree or on the paddock fence. He never bothered any of the livestock, and, most of the time, seemed completely oblivious to the comings and goings around him. We decided to call him George Ow-well, a pun on the author George Orwell.

We never tired of watching George. His size was still awesome, and when he would unfold his powerful wings and silently swoop across the snowy fields, we felt a secret thrill of fear. He never came near us. Although he would let us walk up to him, none of us dared go much closer than five or six feet—he was just too big, and it was unnerving to be watched by two yellow, unblinking orbs.

I read somewhere that the North American Indians believed the arrival of an owl signaled a time of change. Since I have always enjoyed change, I wanted to believe that George signaled some wind of change blowing into my life, especially since he had appeared only a few hours after I had written my Heart's Desire note. This

74

note, written from me to the Lord, lists my desires for the coming year. They invariably involve change in my life. George seemed to physically usher in the possibilities of these changes during the year ahead.

My practice of writing this note on New Year's Eve came after years of burdening myself with New Year's resolutions that I knew I would never keep. The Heart's Desire note is not a resolution; it is an acknowledgement that everything I am and will be comes from the Lord.

First, I write the verse from Psalm 37:4, "Take delight in the Lord, and he will give you the desires of your heart" (RSV). Then, I list what the desires of my heart are for the coming year, seal the envelope, and try to forget all about it. I don't open the note again until the next New Year's Eve. It is always exciting to see how the Lord has given me the desires of my heart—not always in a way that I expect, but always in a way that is tangible. Sometimes, the desire I wrote a year before no longer holds relevance in my life because my life has changed in other ways. Sometimes the desire seems unimportant and trivial compared to what the Lord has been doing throughout the year.

The note also gives me a focal point during the year if I feel that I am being ignored by the Lord. I might remember a desire that I have written down, but I also have to remember that I should be delighting in the Lord. When I do delight in the Lord, my desire generally loses its urgency.

As soon as I saw George swooping across the fields, I thought of the note I had written only a few hours before. The desires were still fresh in my mind, and I mystically thought that George signaled the beginning of their fulfillment. The next year I couldn't remember the contents of the note exactly (that's what makes the New Year's Eve opening so special), but I knew that there were things such as: write another book; meet someone special; and probably, lose ten pounds! Fairly simple desires, but important to me. Their fulfillment was a promised gift of God and a promise that needed only my continuing delight in the Lord to bring to fruition.

I did feel a pang for the lost phone caller. Secretly, I wondered if I had thrown away one of my desires by chasing George around the house. Perhaps, I had thought, this was one item on my list that I already goofed up. I quickly reminded myself that my only worry was to delight in the Lord—my desires would be taken care of. I also reminded myself that when one door closes, another one always opens.

Well, several months passed and it was close to another New Year's Day. So much had happened since George flew into our lives, and I knew that when I opened my letter on New Year's Eve, the desires of my heart will have been fulfilled. I had since met and married "someone special." I had written another book—this one. And yes, I did manage to lose ten pounds!

As for any other desires I might have listed, I am confident that those gifts were given to me as well. Some may not have been in the form I expected; some may not have been as obvious as I would have wished; but in all ways, God honors the promise of the gift of the desires of our hearts. And simply in response to our delighting in the Divine.

Simply? Delighting in the Lord is not always easy. Especially when the dryer breaks down, the cat leaves a mess in the living room, and the kids are having problems at school. That's when the delighting becomes a conscious act of will.

And what is delight? Being pleased with, receiving pleasure from, rejoicing in, luxuriating in, relishing, having a liking for, entering into the spirit of, solacing oneself with, feeling at home with, breathing freely in, basking in the sunshine of, being at ease with, enjoying, treating oneself to, comforting with—not to mention overjoyed, entranced, enchanted, enraptured, transported, fascinated, and finally, one's heart leaping with joy. That list is courtesy of *Roget's Thesaurus* and certainly seems to pin it down a little. I think God would approve.

Like all of the gifts of God, there is a responsibility attached to the desires of our hearts. But what a joyful responsibility this one is: simply to delight.

9

The Gift of Beauty for Ashes

---

*The Spirit of the Lord God is upon me; because the
Lord hath annointed me to . . . appoint unto them
that mourn in Zion, to give unto them beauty
for ashes, the oil of joy for mourning, the
garment of praise for the spirit of heaviness.*
—Isaiah 61:1, 3, KJV

The first day that I saw snow at Stillwater Farm I rushed outside to take a picture of it. The whole area had been magically transformed, and although I know this sounds trite, it was a "winter wonderland." That winter we had very little snow, and I enjoyed the few light dustings that we did receive, each time marveling at the transformation of Stillwater.

At the first sign of snow, I bought cross-country skis for everyone, although we never did get enough snow to actually use them. It did freeze hard, though, and we were able to enjoy skating on the pond.

We had no animals to worry about that first winter, and, consequently, didn't bother about getting out to the barn. I never had to use my snowblower, and, apart from one blowy day, never even shoveled off the steps.

I should have known that it wouldn't last.

The next summer, we bought chickens and donkeys. I had water hooked up from the house to the barn, ordered some hay, greased the snowblower, and sat back smugly. I was ready.

It started to snow in mid-October—just a light dusting, not enough to get excited about. Then, on November 9 (the date sticks in my memory because I had to drive five hundred miles round trip to Toronto that day), it really started to snow. No little pretty flakes drifting down. No picturesque caps on the fence posts. This was *snow!* Within hours every road for miles was blocked solid. School buses brought the children back from school early, businesses closed, and mothers spent a frantic day trying to find mufflers, mittens, and overshoes. (I spent the day affirming my faith: "Please, God, don't let me go off into the ditch here!")

That was the beginning. It snowed pretty well every second day for the rest of the winter. Nathan became an expert at snowblowing. We never saw the pond again after that first snow. If there was a good surface for skating, within hours it was buried deep in the snow, and it would have taken an arena-sized machine to clean it. Instead, the cross-country skis were finally unearthed from the basement, and we discovered the joys of exploring the cedar bush, traversing back fields, and breaking new tracks into the swamp.

We also discovered the joys and frustrations of tending to animals in the deep of winter. First the pipes to the barn froze. That meant carrying water up from the house twice a day. Eventually, I rigged up a baby sled to hold the buckets, but the water would sometimes slosh onto the runners, which would in turn ice up, and the sled would stick fast.

Water left in the barn overnight became frozen solid and had to be chipped out of the buckets in the morning. Hot water alleviated the situation a little, but that meant another trip, carrying the kettle.

The deep snow also covered the donkeys' field, and any small tufts of grass that might have tided them through the day were soon buried. Every morning and evening, we lugged extra bales of hay into the paddock for them.

Of course, if the chickens' eggs weren't picked up promptly from the nests, they froze solid and cracked. Some of the chickens developed frostbite on their combs.

It wasn't fun.

By February, I had had it with the whole business. I would have cheerfully given away Stillwater Farm to the first person who offered me a trip to anywhere sunny. I was tired of shoveling snow, carrying water, feeding animals, and driving on winter roads. Even cross-country skiing lost its charm: the snow was too deep to ski over, and we all got sick of wading knee-deep in the drifts.

At the end of February, we had one monster of a storm that topped all the rest. It snowed steadily for three days. There was no question of going to school or getting to work. Even trekking to the barn was abandoned after an initial trip to make sure that the animals had plenty of food and water to tide them over. There was nothing to do except keep the fires going. We slept a lot, ate a lot, and then slept some more. Occasionally, one or another of us would make a brief foray outside, but the howling winds and driving snow soon forced us back in.

By the third day, the winds had dropped a little, and the snow was confined to brief flurries. It was time to start digging out.

Throughout the storm, I had debated whether or not to start the snowblower to try to keep the path to the barn open. I decided to wait until the whole thing was over and do it in one sweep. It wasn't one of the best decisions I have ever made.

The drifts to the barn were easily four and five feet deep. When you consider that I am just over five feet tall myself, you can appreciate the difficulties that lay ahead. The snowblower chute was set for a maximum of eighteen inches from the ground. I still had three and one-half feet to go. The only way that I could cut a path through the drifts was to lift the chute of the blower up to chew through the top layer, then lift again through the next layer, and so on. It wasn't long before my arms and shoulders began to protest.

During the summer, I had often commented how fortunate we were to have a barn placed a good distance from the house. No problems with odors or flies, I told my friends.

Now, the once-convenient path seemed endless. It took the better part of four hours to clear a narrow pathway to the barn, and there was still the driveway to go!

A thousand times I decided to give up. A thousand times I rued the day I had decided to buy some animals for the barn. And each time, I promised myself that, when this was all over, I would sell the whole lot.

With Nathan and me working in shifts, we did eventually clear both the barn path and the driveway. The animals were fed and watered, the school bus once again stopped at the end of the drive, and I headed out for the highway and work.

But the memory lingered on.

On a beautiful spring morning, I would find myself thinking of the winter just past and the winter to come. The beauty of the morning paled beside the memory of steaming buckets and frozen sled runners. Watching the donkeys browsing in the lush summer meadows, I would find myself thinking of the heavy bales of hay that would be needed for the coming winter.

On the first frosty morning of the next autumn, I felt a stirring of panic as I realized that winter was once again on its icy way. The pipes to the barn would freeze, the fields would be covered with snow, and the chickens' water bucket would be rimmed with ice in the mornings. I dreaded the days to come.

I was losing the joy I had always felt for Stillwater Farm. Where I had once walked down the barn path, praising the Lord for such lovely land and for such beauty all around me, I now saw only the phantom snow drifts, piled high on either side. The beauty of my farm had turned to ashes, and all for a memory.

The same thing happens in so many other areas of our lives. The memory of a lost love overshadows the joy to be found in a new love. The memory of an old hurt builds a barrier that prevents new healing. The memory of a past disappointment clouds the anticipation of an event we have longed for.

But the Lord has promised us the gift of beauty for the ashes; joy for our mourning; praise for heaviness. This is one of the hardest gifts to accept since we must consciously decide to move from the darkness to the light.

Sometimes such an action can only be taken by a sheer act of will. Although sometimes difficult to muster, the desire to leave behind the memories, the mourning, the heaviness is all that is needed to trigger the transformation from dark to light. From the moment that we say, "Take them, Lord, and in their place, fill my life with beauty, joy, and praise," it begins to happen.

And it continues to happen, as long as we remember that it is in our will to refuse to dwell on the past. We must put away the dark thoughts, and even if it means turning them over to the Lord a thousand times a day, eventually they will be gone. The day does come when the ashes and the mourning are no longer in our conscious life. Beauty surrounds us; joy and praise fill our souls.

10

The Gift of the Holy Spirit

*Peter said to them, "Each one of you must turn away
from his sins and be baptized in
the name of Jesus Christ, so that your sins
will be forgiven; and you will receive
God's gift, the Holy Spirit."*

—Acts 2:38

Sometimes we are given gifts that take time to appreciate. I remember a wedding gift I received that illustrates this perfectly. The gift was a beautiful set of matching dessert plates. They were quite old-fashioned in their design: white china with lacy scalloped edges decorated with a pale aquamarine border and a center motif of hand-painted fruits.

I thanked the gift-giver, but in my heart of hearts, I wondered what on earth I was going to do with a set of plates like this. Our apartment at the time was starkly modern: black and white with touches of brilliant blue and green. My china was white, set on a black lacquer table. The napkins, of course, were green and blue stripes. The gift plates just did not go.

Because I seldom used them, the set remained intact. Long after the white china and blue-green napkin set had disappeared and the lacquer table had given way to an oak dining set; when the modern apartment had been replaced with an old manse, full of similarly old furniture; and when I had discovered the beauty of junkyard "antiques," I still had the wedding-gift plates.

It was then that I found their true beauty in the right setting. They were perfect on the oak sideboard, beautiful on the antique lace tablecloth, right at home in the paneled dining room. I used them often and with great pride. I enjoyed their beauty and many times marveled at how absolutely perfect they were for my lifestyle.

Whenever I set them out for another dinner party, I smile as I remember my first reaction to them. And I smile as I realize that the givers had the wisdom to know that young tastes change. I wonder, sometimes, if the givers had seen within me the person I would become: the woman who loves old things, who haunts garage sales, never misses an auction, and is a regular rummager in both church basements and county dumps.

Usually when we receive gifts from God, we know the purpose for which they were given and why they were given to us. But there are some gifts from God that do not have such an obvious purpose in our lives.

One of the gifts we might be given is that of the Holy Spirit, yet we often do not initially appreciate its worth. Ephesians 1:14 tells us that the gift of the Holy Spirit is given to us as a sign of ownership by God. "The Spirit is the guarantee that we shall receive what God has promised his people, and this assures us that God will give complete freedom to those who are his." Although these words have an exciting ring, they seem to have little practical value in our daily lives. Eventually, however, we reach a point in our Christian walk when we begin to hunger for more. We start to ask ourselves, "Is this all there is?" We find ourselves envying those Christians around us who seem to be living a much more exciting, dynamic life.

This is the point at which the Holy Spirit suddenly has some relevance to our lives. We discover that this spirit is the life-giving, power-house of the Christian religion. The Holy Spirit is the source of an incredible array of the spiritual gifts of God.

If we make a quick list of the kinds of gifts of the Spirit that God can grant to us, it can be quite awe-inspiring: the ability to speak God's message; the gifts of service, teaching, sharing, authority, kind-ness, wisdom, knowledge, faith, healing, discern-ment; the abilities to speak in tongues, interpret tongues, work miracles; the vocations of apostles, prophets, evangelists, pastors, teachers, helpers, and leaders; and the gifts of service and of sharing.

Despite this generous list, many of the gifts are misunderstood, ignored, or misused. Sometimes they are seen as badges of Christian achievement, and indeed, many Christians perpetuate this con-ception. We become a society of "haves" and "have nots." I'm sure that God never meant these gifts to create two classes of Christians: those who manifest the gifts of the Spirit, and those who do not. I'm convinced that all of the gifts have a useful purpose in the kingdom.

I remember how I received the gift of tongues. I was praying for a friend of mine, a non-Christian to whom I had been witnessing for some time. It was late at night, and I wanted so hard to pray the right prayer for him. Eventually, I just ran out of words to say; I didn't have the vocabulary to express my deepest desire for him. At this point, I began very quietly to speak in a language unknown to me. I knew that I was still praying for my friend, because I was aware of the general meaning of the words. I felt an incredible sense of relief as my spirit was finally able to speak directly to God without the intervention and interference of my human wishes and desires. That was all—just a deep, quiet conviction that this was a gift of God. I still speak in tongues at times of deep need, at times of joyful praise, or at times when I feel the desire to really communicate again.

Through the gifts of the spirit, we become the powerful Christians that God meant for us to be. We can move forward into the world, unafraid, bold, ready to face any crisis or situation. What an exciting thought!

Have you been asked to teach Sunday school but felt a little inadequate? Pray for the gift of teaching, of evangelism, of authority, of kindness, or of all four.

Have you felt the need to become more involved in your community outreach project? Pray for the gift of service, of sharing, of kindness, of helping.

Have you met people who you feel need the presence of God in their lives, but you don't know how to respond? Pray for the gift of wisdom or of knowledge.

Do you feel you must speak to someone about God? Pray for the gift of speaking God's message with boldness.

Do you feel a burdening need to pray for someone, but don't know how to pray? Ask for the gift of spiritual language—tongues.

Is someone sick? Pray for the gift of healing.

Is someone discouraged? Pray for the gift of encouragement.

No wonder "Old Dirty-Face" would like us to misunderstand the Holy Spirit. No wonder he stirs up controversy and division over the Holy Spirit. Congregations have been isolated and polarized; families have been torn apart; relationships have been destroyed, all because the Holy Spirit was misunderstood.

When we see the Holy Spirit as Agnes Sanford suggests in *The Healing Gifts of the Spirit,* as the "Enabling Gift of Power," we realize just how vital it is to our daily lives. More importantly, we see how vital it can be to the growth of a healthy church.

11

Christmas Every Day

*He gave us his son—will he not also
freely give us all things?*
                    —Romans 8:32

Do you remember how you felt on Christmas morning when you were small? Can you remember those first incredible moments of waking up when you were still groggy with sleep? At first, it felt the same as any other morning, but then there was that wonderful feeling of elation as you realized that this was it—Christmas!

Remember how you felt when you saw the Christmas tree? The incredible wonder as you stared at the packages underneath? Whether there were few or many, the feeling was always the same: anticipation, excitement, surprise, joy, and wonder.

And then there was the actual moment of opening a gift. The thrill of anticipation as you tore the wrappings off. The excitement as you discovered it was "just what you had always wanted."

For the Christian, it's Christmas morning every day. Not just in the sense of Christ born in us daily, but in the very worldly sense of gifts with our name on them, waiting to be opened.

In every moment of our daily lives—times of high elation or times of deepest despair—the Lord has a gift for us. On the mountain and in the valley, the gifts wait, ours for the taking, and ours to use as we need.

They cost us nothing, although each demands responsibility on our part. To take one of God's gifts, open it, and use it is to begin an exciting adventure with the Lord.

If we feel ill at ease in our soul, powerless, drifting with no purpose, we open our gift of the bread of life. The gift is ours. We simply acknowledge Jesus as Savior and Lord of our lives and we can receive it and hunger no more.

If we are full of fears and doubts, tied up in our own worries and anxieties, the gift of the kingdom of God has been promised to us. We simply allow the Lord to free us to enjoy living in the safety of the kingdom.

If we feel that we can make no Christian impact on the world, that our witness is of no use, then we need to accept the gift of eternal life. Knowing that we will never die gives us the courage to step boldly into this world.

If we are overcome with our sinfulness, whether we feel that our sins are great or small, the gift of grace waits for us. We do not earn this gift; we simply accept it.

If we feel that we cannot face the trials that we see ahead of us, we are given the gift of faith to carry us through. We need only believe that the faith we are given is sufficient, and it always is.

If we hurt or those around us are hurting, we are

given the gift of healing. God chooses what and how to heal, but we must accept the gift before any healing can happen.

If we have wishes, hopes, dreams, and long to see them fulfilled, we will receive the gift of the desires of our hearts. In return, we are asked only to delight in the Lord.

If we are bound by our memories, if our spirit is heavy and we mourn for what was, we need to put those memories behind us and accept the beauty, joy, and praise that is our gift.

If we realize that our own knowledge is not enough to sustain us on our Christian walk, we can ask for the gift of wisdom. But we must be prepared to accept the wisdom of the Lord, which often is not the wisdom of this world.

If we realize that there can be more to our Christian lives than what we are living, it is time to accept the gift of the Holy Spirit, opening ourselves to receive the experiences that the Spirit has for us.

To live a triumphant, meaningful, risking, open Christian life, we must ask for and use the gifts of God. We must also say goodbye to our Divine Uncle George, taking our rightful place as children of a generous God, no longer a distant relative depending upon charity from a sometimes bothersome relation.

Patricia Wilson left an editorial job in Toronto to live on rural Stillwater Farm in Spencerville, Ontario. The adjustments that she and her family have experienced provide entertaining and illuminating insights to the spiritual life.

In addition to living on the farm, Patricia Wilson is the Manager of Marketing and Communications for the St. Lawrence Parks Commission, an agency of the government of Ontario. She has previously written *The Daisies Are Still Free* and *Who Put All These Cucumbers in My Garden?*